How Thoughts are Things

The Simple Psychology of How We Turn Thoughts into Things

SWAMI PARAMANANDA

ALIO PUBLISHING GROUP

Print ISBN: 978-1-961959-16-3

E-book ISBN: 978-1-961959-17-0

www.aliopublishing.com

Contents

Preface

The following book briefly and beautifully elaborates on the psychology of thought. *What does that mean?*

By now, many of us are familiar with the phrase "thoughts are things". However: if that statement is true, have you ever wondered **HOW** thoughts actually become things?

This work simply and concisely explains the cause and effect, as well as the connection between conceiving the invisible things we think, and manifesting the very visible things we see.

How Thoughts are Things: The Simple Psychology of Turning Thoughts into Things is a modern restoration of a work written by Swami Paramananda for Vedanta Monthly. Ages ahead of the time period he lived in, Paramananda himself wrote:

"Thoughts produce actions, and actions produce like reactions. Thus: all of our happiness and unhappiness, success and failure, and the endless multiplicity of moods and feelings, are but fruits and flowers from the tree of life, first existing in the seed form of thought."

With the former in mind, please continue reading. Render clear beyond all doubt the why behind cause and effect, as well as the connection between what we think...and what we see.

CHAPTER ONE

Right Thought

Thoughts are things. This simple sentiment so often expressed by us, has far greater significance than we usually attach to it. Our thoughts become concrete things in our life.

Thoughts produce actions, and actions produce like reactions. And so: all our happiness and unhappiness, success and failure, and the endless multiplicity of moods and feelings, are simply fruits and flowers that sprout forth from the tree of life, and exist initially as seed forms of thought.

In The Dhammapada it is written that all that we are is the result of what we have thought. It is founded on our thoughts. It is made up of our thoughts.

If a man speaks or acts with an evil thought, pain follows him as the wheel follows the foot of the ox that draws the carriage. All that we are, is the result of what we have thought. It is founded on our thoughts. It is made up of our thoughts.

When a man speaks or acts with a pure thought, happiness follows him like a shadow that never leaves his side! The entire phenomena and psychology of thought can be summed up in these two ideas: thoughts produce actions; and actions produce like reactions.

As a rule, we do not observe subtle causes, but instead deal largely with effects. For instance, we observe a flower in blossom, or a plant that is withered. However: neither blossoming nor withering happens by chance.

The causes often are hidden due to their abstract quality and subtlety, but they are never separated from all the effects that are produced in the phenomenal world. If we ever experience any happiness, there is a very definite reason for it.

Likewise, whenever we experience unhappiness, there is also a definite reason for it. We are all very interested in doing things that will bring us happiness, and secure our quality of life. But we cannot earn such things merely by the working of our hands, without first creating the foundation of right thought.

In fact, there cannot be any true standard for right living without the basic principle of right thinking. People whose outer life is intensely active are inclined to misunderstand the significance of the subject, and may imagine that giving too much eminence to thought will likely lead to morbid thinking.

Such beliefs are typically a sign of surface observations. Thought does not necessarily mean inaction. On the contrary, thought generates action in both the mind and the body.

This can be easily verified by every individual person. Whenever we are engaged in concentrated thought, it immediately produces a certain vibration, which results in making the body either tense, or mobile.

Sometimes our thoughts cause us to feel dull; heavy; draped in melancholy. At other times, they generate such tremendous force that we feel we are not even touching the ground.

When we are walking, if the mind is charged with some powerful thought, it carries the body. Unconsciously we walk faster. The weight of the body is lifted by the velocity of thought.

These are not fantasies. These are actual facts; but often, they pass by unobserved - and that is why we tend to lay greater stress on action than on thought. If we are not able to understand the fundamental value of right thinking, then all our high ideals will be of little avail.

No one can create great things merely with his hands or his material assets. He must be sustained by noble thoughts. Thought is most potent in molding our destiny.

Even so: do not imagine that all we have to do is to sit and think, and everything will come right to us. That will bring us nothing. It is inconsistent.

If a man is animated by lofty thoughts and high aspirations, what is the most immediate thing for him to do? He seeks to express them. He strives to make them real.

Thought and action are inseparable, and they must always be inseparable...just like with any tree, and its root.

You cannot conceive of a tree living and flowering if severed from its root. So it is with our life and all its multiplicity of thoughts and feelings.

CHAPTER TWO

There are no Accidents

E very man who turns his attention inward, sooner or later, must realize that there is no such thing as accidents. It is only the person of limited understanding – the individual who does not see beyond the scope of the phenomenal – who says *"it happened by chance"* or *"I just acted out of impulse"*.

All that we do *is* the result of certain, definite, specific lines of thought.

Not very long ago there was an article in a magazine; a discussion in regards to a criminal case. A judge had sentenced a 17 year-old who had been arrested after an attempted bank robbery. Many thought the youth should have been shown more mercy.

They argued that the boy was ignorant; that he had acted on impulse. The judge cross-questioned that youth, and found that it was not at all a momentary lapse – that for months, the boy had brooded deliberately over the very idea of robbing a bank.

The idea came to him first as a simple thought. Then it was gradually grounded into his very being, became a part of his life, and when the outer opportunity was offered...he offered himself up and fell into it.

Our happiness is not through chance, and our unhappiness is not through chance. It is better to understand this from the very beginning, because it will help us to eliminate unrest from our own minds, and to free the minds of others.

When we live only on the surface of life, then we feel the unrest in ourselves and in the world. And only when we view things solely from the surface, do we say it was an accident. There is always a deep, underlying cause.

Chance is the notion of idle people. They are constantly looking for miracles; and miracles never come to them. Miracles come only to those who are awakened; who are pure and exalted in spirit. They alone can perceive what the world calls miracles.

CHAPTER THREE

Quality of Mind

When things go wrong with us – when we allow ourselves to be mentally disturbed – we find *many* excuses.

We explain that it was because of other people, their thoughts, their influence upon us, or their actions. *He abused me. She beat me. He defeated me. She wrapped me.* So we complain.

When we realize that nothing can have any disturbing or harmful effect upon us; once we are purified within, then any idea of complaining fades away from us. If we hold hateful or unkind thoughts, unhappiness will never cease for us. Hatred will never cease.

Happiness has nothing to do with how much we have, or how little. It does not depend on where we are placed, or in what circumstances. Material conditions will not secure us our peace. Such matters are determined entirely by the quality of one's mind.

The small mind sees the limited. The big mind sees the unlimited. The vision of limitation is our own creation, and the vision of the unlimited is a quality of our unfoldment.

We have heard this many times. We may have to hear it many more times, because we do not always here with the inner ear. Our inner life does not always respond to these sayings.

It is a question of unfoldment, and the unfoldment of our real nature is not possible, unless it begins from within. Outer things we can have done for us by others, but the inner things we **must** do for ourselves.

In modern life we forget this. We like to have people think things out for us. But there is no one who can think for us, and make us wise. It is a great tragedy when we are overcome by such spiritual lethargy.

There are certain invariable laws. There is, for example, the law of compensation. It plainly states that if a man speaks or acts with an evil thought, pain follows him like the wheel follows the foot of the ox that draws the carriage.

Here, compensation does not mean merely reward and punishment. It means that everything which comes to us – good, evil, and in between – comes only because we ourselves have made it possible. We sow the seeds by our own thoughts.

CHAPTER FOUR

The Tempter (the Ego)

He who lives looking for pleasure only – his senses uncontrolled, excessive in his food, idle and weak – will certainly find himself overthrown by the tempter, just as the wind throws down the split branches of a weak tree.

What is this tempter? Here is a point of dogma. Some people believe in a "personal" devil. The devil does exist; but, in the individual himself.

In India, they call it the ego. There is no enemy so potent, so hostile, so difficult to conquer as the ego. We may have all the blessings the world can give. But if the ego is rampant and goes unchecked, we shall know neither rest nor happiness.

Ego always demands. If we have little, it wants more. If we have more, it wants *everything*. It sets us on fire.

Ambition is like that as well; it consumes us. We can have no chance for peace or stability, so long as we follow those lower propensities. Now how do they first fasten their holds on us? ***Through our thoughts.***

We have the power to transform our life by changing our mode of thinking. In The Upanishads, one of India's most ancient scriptures, this is given very simply and directly:

"Mind alone is the cause of man's bondage; and mind alone is the cause of his liberation."

We are born with certain tendencies; with the natural spirit of nobility...or the reverse. Whenever we say we inherit our nature from our parents, we are giving a very unsatisfactory explanation.

It is the individual alone who sowed the seeds of good or evil in the soil of their life – and not this small span of life necessarily.

CHAPTER FIVE

The Life Beyond the Body

There is a connecting link with other existences. Our life did not begin with, or in, this particular physical body. Our whole evolution and freedom do not depend solely upon these few short years of living.

Our book of destiny will never be complete, nor shall we be able to read one complete line of it, until we connect the present existence with what has gone before. Then, we shall see even more fully than we do now, that if a man thinks kind

thoughts and performs kind acts – if his inten-
tions are pure – happiness will follow him faith-
fully like a shadow, and it will never leave him.

You may deny this. You may say that the good
suffer; that they are often cheated and robbed,
or that they sometimes meet with calamity. That
may be so...but they never suffer as much as the
ignorant.

Whatever we earn by our own merit, that no one
can take from us. We see this at every turn.

A noble soul may be deprived of many of the
blessings of this material existence. His enemies
may torment him, but they cannot touch what is
his birthright. They cannot rob him of his peace.

A man who commits a crime after heavy contem-
plation of evil thoughts, tries to escape from pain,
but cannot. Where do we feel pain the most? In
the mind.

We cannot do something harmful to another without suffering ourselves. That is the reason the Bible teaches to "love thy neighbor as thyself."

CHAPTER SIX

Love Your Neighbor

Why should one love one's neighbor as one's self? In the Vedic Upanishad, the wise sage tells his disciple:

"my son, verily thou art thine own neighbor."

From the point of view of the soul, we cannot rob someone without robbing ourselves.

We rob our own dignity, we rob our own peace; we rob the finer things in our life. (Here the word "rob" is synonymous with "remove".)

We cannot harm another without harming ourselves as well.

We cannot cheat the Greater Law.

A wise person not only never wants to evade the law; he wishes to benefit by it.

CHAPTER SEVEN

Thought is a Power

T hought is a power; a power for good, and a power for evil. If we do not direct the mind through the proper channels of kindness, wisdom, love, and all things that are constructive, it will find other avenues that will perhaps prove destructive.

Here enters our responsibility. You may say: *"everything is done through Divine Will, so why should we bear responsibility?"*

If we have reached the point of surrender and vision where we can perceive The Divine Will, then we are rid of responsibility.

But, there are very few of us who can sincerely say that we abide by The Divine Will; that we have no individual desires. So long as we have desires, so long as we have ambition – so long as we involve ourselves with any of these emotions – we must direct them through the right channels.

Every intelligent human being knows the law of life: **As a man thinks...so is he**. It *is* the supreme secret.

To possess the knowledge of it gives the greatest power. But if we know it only superficially, it does not benefit us. How few there are among us today who are able to apply it!

We all know that if we surround ourselves with thoughts of love and purity, they safeguard us; they build a tremendous barricade of protection around us. And yet, in spite of our mental grasp of this fact, when someone has offended or injured us, we allow these incidents to take over our conscious thoughts.

If we allow our mind to be filled with evil thoughts and sordid feelings; if we allow it to be clouded by envy, jealousy and anger...can we expect to find peace?

CHAPTER EIGHT

Doubt VS Affirmation

The more we brood, the more our mind becomes colored by our brooding. It gradually poisons our entire being. Yet the same mind which feels itself incapable of anything good or lofty can become potent, victorious; its own liberator.

Sometimes we become hypnotized by the idea of weakness and inability. No one can help us so long as we allow ourselves to remain under that influence. Its antidote is to have the opposing idea: "I am strong."

Even if we cannot say it with conviction, if we are in earnest – if our spirit is desirous of throwing off the weakness – we shall find that gradually, like the sun, it will dispel all the dark clouds, and deliver us strength.

Sometimes, this is called an affirmation. It creates an opportunity for the mind to make contact with that which is all-powerful.

It is not by dwelling on weakness that we get rid of weakness. It is by dwelling on strength that we become strong. It is by dwelling on light that we conquer darkness. It is by dwelling on wisdom that we overcome ignorance.

CHAPTER NINE

How We Become Spiritual

No one can give us salvation. You may disagree with that assessment. If we follow religion, some will say, we shall be saved. But following religion means living religion.

It is not by professing creeds or attaching importance to rituals that we become spiritual. It is when our life and our belief correspond.

It is when there is no inconsistency: mind and mouth working together, thought and action running harmoniously. That is the whole, healthy psychology of existence.

Today, particularly in the Western Hemisphere, people have become interested in what some call Practical Psychology. It is indeed most practical; but do not for a moment think that true psychology of thought can be lowered to the plane of petty desires...

...or that it can be used to satisfy the longing for a new hat, or a new coat; or that by sitting down and concentrating, one can acquire prosperity or some other small end. Not quite!

True psychology brings an expanded consciousness. We testify to our faith by our actions; by our very being. You may ask: are we capable of this? We are just as capable of it as something small and insignificant.

The same amount of energy we expend in idle talk, or in imagining things which never come to a head, if concentrated and directed, would give us power to accomplish mighty and magnificent things.

CHAPTER TEN

Thoughts Becomes Realities

E very thought becomes a reality – kind thoughts and unkind thoughts. This should not carry with it any idea of doom, even to the selfish and ignorant.

We can redeem ourselves no matter where we now stand, or how we stand. We can remold our life to a great extent. Some may think it is an egotistic notion that a man should take on the responsibility of molding his own life.

If he thinks that he alone does it; if he does not take account of a higher Power, it **will** be egotistical, and he is bound to fail. But he cannot be egotistic if his motive is pure, if his heart is kind; if he has a deep sense of consecration. These feelings will lead him to the higher ideal.

Self-dejection is the greatest enemy we can possibly have. We all should remember that we each have the spark of Divinity within us. Whatever one's personal life philosophy or religion may be, makes no difference there whatsoever.

There is no one who does not have a faith, call it what he will. Let him cling to that. Let him fasten his whole being to that, and he will be inspired to redeem himself.

The power of inspiration is within us, and we must awaken it. The man who is hungry and thirsty for happiness will find it, if he creates a foundation of pure thoughts and noble ideals.

If we have that foundation within us, even though we are condemned and ridiculed by the whole world, we shall walk in safety. If we do not have it, the whole world can befriend us and we will still feel unhappy and unfulfilled.

Pain follows him who acts with selfish purposes. Happiness follows him who acts with pure motive. These two eternal principles are ever before us. They are simple, direct, scientific, logical, and true.

We need people of character more than men of action. It is very dangerous to enter into this arena of activity without meditative thought. When a man plunges into the field of action without coordinated thought, what is typically the result? He does things which later have to be undone.

This translates into waste, and waste means not only loss of time and energy, but moral dejection. Therefore, we must think first, deep down within our own being, and to our thoughts add earnest reflection.

There is no human being so depraved, or beyond reach, that he or she cannot look up to their Creator. This process of keeping our channel clear and free, so that we may have unbroken access to The Highest, is the very sum and substance of religion. All other things, by comparison, are side issues.

Love brings love. Kindness brings kind feelings. If we are capable of sending love from our hearts, should we not then aim to gather good results from the tree of life?

If we approach someone with kindness, and are met with no response, let us not be discouraged or faint-hearted. There is no haste in the world of the spirit.

Eternity is before us, and behind us, and all around us. When our heart is made pregnant with such lofty thoughts, we shall reap the rich fruition of true spiritual blessing.

This is the most pure, essential psychology of thought.

About the Author

Swami Paramananda (1884–1940) was a poet, a mystic, and one of India's first teachers to spread the Vedanta philosophy & religion throughout the USA.

On February 5th, 1884, Suresh Chandra Guhathakurta was born as the youngest son of a prestigious Guhathakurta family in Banaripara village. His father, Ananda Mohan Guha-Thakurta, was an effective advocate for women's education - a legacy he would pass on to his sons.

Suresh met his teacher, Vivekananda, who was the foremost disciple of Ramakrishna - and the first swami to teach in America - at the age of 17. Paramananda was sent to New York in 1906 to assist the city's Vedanta Society. He lived and taught there until 1909, when the Vedanta Centre of Boston was established.

In 1909 he founded the Message of the East, the first Vedanta-themed periodical published in the USA. For 55 years the magazine offered articles and commentary on all religions. He also authored translations of the Bhagavad Gita and The Upanishads, along with copious books and publications.

He founded four non-sectarian ashramas (two in the USA; two in Calcutta) with a female majority that remain active today. Much like his teacher, Paramananda believed in equality between men and women. Throughout the entire history of the community he helped grow, women were accorded positions of leadership in all areas.

He lectured across the United States, Europe and Asia for 34 years until his death in 1940. Paramananda's pioneering contributions to the spiritual community continue to stand beyond compare.

Also by ALJO Publishing

The Little Blue Book (El Librito Azul):

Metaphysics in Simple Terms

by Conny Méndez

THE HIDDEN SECRET OF GOD:

The Bible Decoded

by Neville Goddard Volume One

The Mystery of Christ:

The Bible Decoded

by Neville Goddard Volume Two

Karmic Astrology:

Mastering Key Life Lessons

for All 12 Zodiac Signs

by Copper Moon

Finding Your Voice:

A Practical Self Help Guide to Stop Stuttering

by Dominick Barbara

Meditation in 7 Pages

by Robe Chatman

Spirit Speaks Louder Than Words:

an unconventional memoir

by Robe Chatman